Hey You! C'mere

a poetry slam

by

Elizabeth Swados

illustrated by

Joe Cepeda

Arthur A. Levine Books

An Imprint of Scholastic Inc.

Table of

Amelia

Sis

Ratchit

Contents

Jacob

Daria

Josh

Mattie

Banging on a garbage can,
Bam bam bam.
Mattie says it's time
For a poetry slam.

Everybody's talkin' poems!

Everybody's laughin' poems!

Sis is eatin' poems!

Josh is drinkin' poems!

Amelia's wearin' poems on her feet!

The sky is filled with poems!

And Jacob rides a poem on the sidewalk

While Doria pours poems out of a pitcher.

Ratchit throws a poem at your back, ouch!

It's poem time, you have poems circling around your head,

You've got a poem in your pocket,
A poem on your tongue, did you know that?
You can be the poet and you can be the poem too.
Yesssss!

Tough Kids

"Hey you, c'mere,"

Says the kid down the street.

I hear his big mean feet.

"Hey you, c'mere,"

His voice is tough,

And his pushes are rough,

"Hey you, c'mere,

Whatsa matter witcha,

You sposta do what I

Tell ya to do.

I'll beatch ya if ya don't!"

I turn to him

With my sweetest grin,

And say,

"Hey you, guess what? I <u>won't</u>."

Now, you were brave with that bully.
If it had been me,
I would've just cried my eyes out!

A Good

You may wonder why
But sometimes I like to cry.
I like the sound,
Haaw, haaw,
Wah, wah,
Eeee eee,
Hiccup cough sniff,
Hiccup cough sniff.
It's got a beat to it,
I like the taste of tear,
Lick, lick, lick.
Mom says, "What's the
        matter, dear?"
Dad holds out his arms and says,
"Come here, come here."
It's not a bad deal,
Haaw wahee yaw,

Cry

To break down and howl,
To howl like a seal,
Aw aw aw aw,
To be like a bird and
Caw caw caw.
Crying can be really fun,
Except when you're hurt
    or you're the one
Getting bopped.
Then it's like a waterfall,
And you can't stop.

But there's no time to cry, guys. Get into the summer mood.

12

Summer

Tsss

Summer sounds,

Tsss

Concrete and heat,

Sneakered feet on tar,

Stepping on a melted candy bar,

Squish

Crunch, crunch

Gravel on the street,

Whoosh

Hydrant waterfall,

Zzzzt

The sun's an orange basketball,

Bonk bonk

Summer sounds,
And then the
Summer's gone.

Storm

Boom! Thunder!

Boom! Thunder!

First the lightning,

Crack!

It's frightening.

Then the **BOOM**,

Thunder,

Outside my room.

BOOM, the thunder,

And the rain pours,

Like nails on the roof,

And **POOF!**

Out go the lights.

Interruption! Interruption! Here comes a storm!

What a night.
BOOM! Thunder!
Night of fright,
Night of wonder,
BOOM! Thunder.

Aunt

I'm going to kiss you,

Smooch you,

Koo-kootchie koo you.

I'm going to snuggle you,

Huggle you,

Niggle you and *nuggle* you,

Cuddle you too.

I'm going to pinch you,

Nuzzle you,

Fizzle you and *fuzzle* you.

Oh no! Not Aunt Evelyn!

Evelyn

Don't run away.

Oooh I could squeeze you,

Take a bite from your cute cheek,

Nibble all your fingers up,

And love you till you shriek.

Uh-Oh

Chomp chomp,
I'm naht suwposed to tawlk
Wid moy moudth fulled.
Chomp chomp,
Itds bayad mahnners.
Chomp chomp.

21

Here we are, but we're never gonna get in.
My Great Granma won't hear us.

Great Granma

Great Granma's kind of deaf – Ay?

Great Granma takes short breaths – oof

Great Granma's elbow creaks – eeh

Great Granma's eyes can leak – yuk

Great Granma laughs with a wheeze – hyee

Great Granma gets mad when you tease – DANG

Great Granma sometimes mumbles – mmm

Great Granma sings through her nose – nana

Great Granma likes to doze – zzz

Great Granma sometimes forgets – Who?

Great Granma has not one regret – NO SIR!

Great Granma likes to tell stories – Blah blah

Sometimes her stories are boring – zzz

Great Granma loves everyone – Bless you all

She calls us her daughters and sons – My you're tall!

Great Granma's as good as they get – Hooray!

Great Granma has not one regret – NO SIR!

Mr. Befuddled

Finally, it's Mattie's uncle.
Hey, Uncle Lester,
can you let us in?

Mr. Befuddled – ah – well – yes – no,

Ask him a question, oh dear, ah ho,

Mr. Befuddled can't say yes or no,

Hm, gee, oh my gosh, I don't know,

 gosh, I don't know,

Oh gosh oh gee oh me oh my,

Oh well, I – um – uh – well mm sigh,

Ah ooh ah um uh well, uh oh um yikes,

 gosh oh me oh la oh la,

Mr. Befuddled can't say yes or no.

The Tele

Mom, I brought the poets home!
If she's like my mom she'll never hear you!

phone

When the telephone rings,

It's just like my mommy sings,

She goes:

Yeah, uh huh, uh huh.

When the telephone rings,

Who knows what news it brings?

'Cause my daddy goes,

Hmmm? Is that so?

I can't wait to answer the telephone

On my own, on my own

'Cause then I'll know

What the hmmm and the oh

Is an answer to.

The: Really? You do?

And I can make some answers too.

Right back to that silly phone.

Thank you.
Good-byyyyeee!

Spaghetti

Schlump one long piece of spaghetti,

I'm gonna get it, yep I'm ready,

Breathe in deep,

Here I go,

Schlurp, schlurp, schlurp, schlurp,

Oh no,

How long does this spaghetti grow?

This one piece just goes and goes,

Schlurp, schlurp, schlurp, schlurp,

Schlurp, schlurp, schlurp, schlurp,

29

It's wrapped around my elbows,

It's tangled in my toes,

It doesn't seem to stop,

It's going up my nose,

I'm covered with meat sauce,

I better take a bath,

That's the longest piece of spaghetti

I've ever, ever,

Ever, ever

Had.

Silly

One of my favorite games
Is making up silly names
Mr. Grub T. Mudstuck, Diane Doobey Doo,
Fineas Figmuff and Tina Tutoo,
Teacup O'Hara, Tushi O'Lay,
Flutfarf, Zegba, and Snarky McKay,
Flubba Dubba Zinga Dinga,
Harken, Larken Sputzey Fritter,

I'm spaghettied out. Let's play a game — the dumbest game I know.

Names

Bubby and Tubby Zarcofsky,
Pudding Blatt Bearallapopsky,
Mr. and Mrs. Blurpglopyahoo,
Grinspok, Jijigern, Yuggle Face Magoo,
And if these names aren't silly enough for you,
Make some yourself,
you *blubba checkoo.*

Monsters

I've checked the inside of my closet,

I've searched under my bed,

I don't know where that *ooh ooh*

Comes from,

Is that the sound of the dead?

Ooh Ooh Ooh Ooh

What a low, sad cry,

It could be the wind in the trees,

But why does it sound like a ghostly sigh?

Ooh Ooh Ooh Ooh

And sometimes *Ee ee ee,*

Wait—stop—shhh.

What's that howl?

Oooooooooooooooooooooooooooooooooooooohhhhh

Is there a spirit flying around
And is it calling me?
If only it weren't so dark in here,
I could meet it face-to-face,
I'd say, "Come on, stop haunting me,
Go and find your own dang space!"
But I'm supposed to be in bed,
And I hear that mournful cry,
Ooh Ooh Ooh Ooh
Someone's crying
And I don't know why.

I'm so scared . . .

What's that crash?

hhhhhhhhhhhhhhhhhhhhhh!!!!!!!!!!!!!!!!!!!!!!!!!!

Me

Me me me me
No one else but me!
Me me my mine
No one else could shine so fine!
Me me me me, mine mine mine mine,
Number one all of the time.
Numero Uno! Yo! It's me,
I'm the one I want to be,
Me myself me and I
I'm no one else, don't want to try.

First of first, most of most,

I'm myself and I don't boast,

Me me now and me me then,

Me myself and me again,

I'm myself and I don't boast,

Me to me from coast to coast.

Group: Hey you, c'mere.

Mattie: Why you give us a rough time? We're gonna get you back with rhythm and rhymin'.

Josh: We wouldn't pay a dime to see your show of tough stuff.

Group: It's enough!

Amelia: You sneak up on us. You think we're weak?

Doria: Hey,   we got camaraderie and poetry and you are the freak show.

You may be a big shot.

Jacob: Who won't share his words
and his stories with us.

Group: It's your loss.

Mattie: That's da cost. Hey, you can
shake yo' fist.

Jacob: But scarin' us is history.

Sis: We're bigger—we've grown.

Amelia: Whereas you—

Group: Hey you, over dere. You're alone.

Ratchit: Uh . . . uh . . . oh . . . my . . .

But we've got each other.
What have you got?

Sorry

I'm sorry sorry sorry.

So sorry oh so very sorry,

Very very sorry, so very very sorry,

So sad and sorry sad and sorry sorry,

Oh so sad and oh so sorry very very sad,

And very very sorry I was so stupid and

Now I'm stupid sad and sorry, stupid sorry

Sad and very sorry, sorry sorry. It was stupid

And I'm sorry, so very sad and very sorry,

I was selfish and stupid

And I am so sorry oh so

Very very sad and sorry for

Being selfish and stupid. I'm sad.

And sorry. I'm sorry.

Give me one more chance.
One more poem to share.

Hey, okay.
Grudges take
too much time. C'mon!

Ice Cre

I got some ice cream,
Slurp, slurp, slurp,
All around my tongue,
Lick, lick, lick,
Gotta beat the sun,
Slurp, slurp, slurp,
Or it'll drip,
Lick, lick, lick,
Here comes my dog,
Slurp, slurp, slurp,
Gotta give her some,
Lick, lick, lick,
Look at her tongue,
Lick, lick, lick,
So pink and slick,
Drip, drip, drip,
Now it's almost gone,
Slurp, slurp, slurp,
Right down to the cone,
Crunch, crunch, crunch,

Don't wanna miss a drop,
Drip, drip, drip,
I'll lick till there's none,
Crunch, slurp, drip, crunch, gone.

The Secret

Psst psst

I've got a little secret,

I want to tell you,

Psst psst

Shhh shhh

I love you,

I do,

I do,

I *doo doo doo bee doo*

Do!

Text copyright © 2002 by Elizabeth Swados
Illustrations copyright © 2002 by Joe Cepeda
All rights reserved. Published by Arthur A. Levine Books, a division of Scholastic Inc.,
Publishers since 1920. SCHOLASTIC and the LANTERN LOGO are trademarks
and/or registered trademarks of Scholastic Inc.
No part of this publication may be reproduced, stored in a retrieval system,
or transmitted in any form or by any means, electronic, mechanical, photocopying,
recording, or otherwise, without written permission of the publisher. For information
regarding permission, write to Scholastic Inc., Attention: Permissions Department,
557 Broadway, New York, NY 10012.

LIBRARY OF CONGRESS CATALOGING-IN-PUBLICATION DATA
Swados, Elizabeth.
Hey you! C'mere: a poetry slam/by Elizabeth Swados;
illustrated by Joe Cepeda   p.   cm.

ISBN-13: 978-0-439-09257-9
ISBN-10: 0-439-09257-4
1. City and town life—Juvenile poetry. 2. Children's poetry, American.
[1. American poetry.] I. Title: Hey you! C'mere!. II. Cepeda, Joe, ill.
III. Title. PS3569.W17 H49 2002   811'.54—dc21   2001029260
10 9 8 7   08 09 10 11 12
Printed in Singapore 46
First edition, March 2002

The poems were set in Senza Medium, with titles in Oogabooga Irregular.
The individual voices were set in Clubhouse.
The art for this book was created using oil paints.
Book design by Marijka Kostiw

To Josh, Mattie, and Doria,
my Goof Children.
—E. S.

For Juana and Julian,
the poetry in my life.
—J. C.